782.81 Powers, Bill
PO
       Behind the scenes
       of a Broadway
       musical

DATE			

Behind the Scenes of a Broadway Musical

Behind the Scenes of a Broadway Musical

by Bill Powers

CROWN PUBLISHERS, INC. NEW YORK

Thanks to producers John Davis and Sheldon Riss.
Special thanks to Maurice Sendak and Sheldon Fogelman
for letting me spend such a happy time on Avenue P.

The text of this book is set in 12 point Primer.
The illustrations are black-and-white photographs.
Designed by Lucy Martin Bitzer

Library of Congress Cataloging in Publication Data
Powers, Bill.
Behind the scenes of a Broadway musical.
Photographic essay.
Summary: Describes the Broadway musical production of "Really Rosie"
through all stages of preparation from planning and rehearsals to previews
and opening night.   1. Musical revue, comedy, etc.—New York (State)—New
York—Juvenile literature.   2. Musical revue, comedy, etc.—New York (State)
—New York—Pictorial works.   3. King, Carole. Really Rosie. [1. Musical re-
vue, comedy, etc.   2. King, Carole. Really Rosie.   3. Sendak, Maurice.
4. Theater—Production and direction]   I. Title.
ML3930.A2P7   782.81'07   82-2514
ISBN: 0-517-54466-0

To
Patricia Birch and
the kids in the cast

Contents

CHAPTER

1

Planning the Play

Nine young actors were lined up on the stage, their faces stretched in grins, top hats waving in the air. The opening night audience in the packed theater was grinning back, clapping in time to the music. The cast bowed and the audience burst into applause. The first performance of Maurice Sendak's *Really Rosie* was over. After all the hard work it seemed like a magic moment. The cast stood erect again, looked at each other and smiled, and bowed again.

Five weeks earlier, the warm lights that lit the actors' faces were still on the shelves. The colorful scenery that surrounded the actors did not exist. Neither did the costumes they wore nor the top hats they were waving above their heads. Five weeks earlier, the stage they were standing on was an empty space.

2

Really Rosie tells the story of how a group of kids on a Brooklyn street spend a hot, boring summer day. With nothing to do, they look to Rosie to entertain them. Rosie has a dream of becoming a movie star and makes up the plot of a movie about her rise to stardom—and her search for her long-lost brother, Chicken Soup (who is really not lost, but hiding in a large cardboard box). All the kids audition for her movie as Rosie relates the story of Chicken Soup's disappearance, and at the end of the play, Rosie rewards them all with parts in the "movie of her life."

Maurice Sendak shows the cast a poster advertising the play.

The first musical version of *Really Rosie* was presented as an animated cartoon TV special in 1975, based on Maurice Sendak's children's book *The Sign on Rosie's Door* and the four volumes in his *Nutshell Library*. The music was written by Carole King, with lyrics by Sendak. Three years later, Maurice Sendak and director-choreographer Patricia Birch were brought together by the well-known producer Stuart Ostrow. This time a longer version of the play, with live actors, was presented by the Music Theater Lab in Washington, D.C. John Davis and Sheldon Riss, who was the executive producer of the TV film, saw the play and decided to bring it to New York. The Music Theater Lab production was done without costumes or scenery. In New York, the musical would be given its first full-scale professional production.

Right away Riss and Davis began a search for one or more individuals to provide money for the Broadway production. With a cast of eleven actors and a five-piece band, *Really Rosie* would not require the huge amount of money needed for a large Broadway musical, but the presentation of any musical is expensive. Enough money would have to be raised to pay salaries and to pay for the scenery, costumes, lights, band, theater rental, advertising, and printing of posters and tickets, with enough left over to get the play through rehearsals and two or three weeks of performances. After that, ticket sales would have to support the play or more money would have to be raised for it to continue being performed.

Riss and Davis raised the money and set up a production company to handle the business end of the play, but there was a delay until a theater could be found. Finally, in the summer of 1980, the producers signed a contract with the Chelsea Theater Center for use of a theater for both rehearsals and performances, and work on the production began.

Producers John Davis (top) *and Sheldon Riss*

Press agent Shirley Herz

As soon as the theater was found and an opening date set, the producers hired a press agent to help draw an audience. The press agent is responsible for writing a notice about the play, called a press release. The press release describes the play and who wrote it, the director and producers, the actors and designers, the theater, and the opening date.

Releases are sent to newspapers, magazines, and radio and TV stations with the hope that some mention of the play will appear in print or over the air. The press agent also tries to arrange interviews for the actors on TV or radio or in the newspapers.

For most Broadway plays an advertising campaign is planned and the first ads appear in newspapers weeks before the play opens. It is hoped that the interest in the play generated by any publicity, interviews, or advertising will result in a big advance sale of tickets.

A large advance sale for a play is important, not only because it brings in money, but because it can mean the life or death of a production, especially if the critics' reviews are not good. Some Broadway plays close after only one performance because of poor reviews. But others survive because their advance sale lets the play run long enough for theatergoers to decide for themselves whether the play is worth seeing. Even after a play opens, the press agent will continue publicizing it to help the production reach as wide an audience as possible.

With any play it is up to the producer to hire the creative people to stage the play. He or she will hire a director, costume designer, set designer, lighting designer, a choreographer to stage the dances, and a musical director—and backing up the creative staff, stage managers, technicians, and stagehands to run the show.

Long before rehearsals begin, the producer and the director hold a series of meetings with the writer and composer and the rest of the creative staff and carefully plan every phase of the production. At these meetings the director presents his or her concept of how the play should look on stage. The story, or "book," may be rewritten and new songs and lyrics added to improve the show. And the look of the scenery, costumes, and lighting will be designed to serve the director's vision of the finished production.

While the designers begin work in their studios on the scenery, lighting, and costumes, the director and choreographer hold auditions for the singers and dancers trying out for parts in the play.

For many years, the cast of a musical play was ordinarily made up of actors who sang and dancers who only danced. But lately, actors who sing are called on to dance and dancers are often asked to sing. This has forced performers to try to develop both skills. For *Really Rosie* the dancing was not as important as the singing and acting, so during auditions the emphasis was on finding young actors who could sing well. Pat Birch, who directed the Music Theater Lab production, would teach them what little dancing there was to learn.

In casting a musical play, the producer or the director's assistants describe to a casting agent the characters in the play, and the agent will send to the auditions actors he or she feels will fit those characters.

Auditions are a little like a contest, with the director, producer, writer, composer, and musical director acting as judges. The actor will usually sing a song he or she has been practicing as an audition piece. If the director and the others like what they hear, the actor will then be asked to read a part of the script. If the actor reads well, the director might give him or her one of the songs from the show to take home and learn and the actor would be given a "call-back." This can happen again and again until the actor either gets the part or is let go.

In the auditions, the director is not just trying to find talented actors and singers, but actors whose looks and personalities fit the characters in the play and who are talented enough to make the characters

Director-choreographer Patricia Birch

April Lerman and Tisha Campbell (opposite), *two of the kids in the cast*

come to life on the stage. Proper casting is probably the single most important element in the production of a play, and it can be a long, hard process.

The casting of *Really Rosie* took a long time. With the help of musical director Joel Silberman, Pat Birch and her assistants auditioned more than 150 children for the six main characters in the play and for a smaller part, the Lion.

Through long hours of auditions and call-backs, the choices were narrowed down until the roles were filled by those actors director Birch felt would bring special qualities to the play and reflect the spirit of Sendak's characters.

The role of Rosie was won by Tisha Campbell, who was eleven years old; Kathy, by April Lerman, also eleven; Pierre, by B. J. Barie, eight; Johnny, by Wade Raley, eight; Alligator, by Joey LaBenz IV, seven; and Chicken Soup, by Jermaine Campbell, Tisha's brother, also aged seven. The part of the Lion was won by Matthew Kolmes, who would fill in for the other actors whenever necessary. Ruben Cuevas, aged seven, wasn't hired until the third week of rehearsals. He would replace, or understudy, Jermaine Campbell in the part of Chicken Soup and, along with Lara Berk and Matthew Kolmes, double as one of the Neighborhood Kids. The script also called for the voices of two mothers. Those parts would be played by assistant stage managers Bibi Humes and Alison Price.

Though very young, most of the cast had a lot of professional experience. Tisha was singing professionally before she entered grade school, B.J. had a nightclub act, April had played in the touring company of the hit show *Annie*, Jermaine had turned professional when he was five, and Wade and Matthew had acted in a number of professional productions.

CHAPTER
2

Rehearsals Begin

The first day of rehearsals arrives. After all the effort spent in raising money and finding a theater, after the auditions, production meetings, and delays, the director and cast get back to the important thing, which is the play. Everyone has been reading and studying it, but now, on September 9, they will sit down for the first time as a company and listen to the words and music together.

Really Rosie was a professional production, so the cast and stage managers filled out forms for medical benefits and life insurance. Then the union representative explained to them the medical benefits and union rules concerning rehearsal hours and days off.

Generally after union business is taken care of, the director, playwright, and composer will join the actors and stage managers around a table or in a circle of chairs for the first reading of the play. The musical director sits at the rehearsal piano, ready to play. It is a little like joining hands and wishing each other luck. Very often this inspires the cast. The play takes on a life in the first reading that will not be seen again until long hours of rehearsal and hard work bring it back.

The first reading of the play

Pat Birch asks the cast to think about their characters.

The empty stage of the Chelsea Theater

While the director influences all the elements in the production, such as the lighting, set design, and costumes, fulfilling them is left up to the designer hired for each job. The director's main function is to rehearse the actors and get them ready to perform.

It looks like fun and sometimes it is, but rehearsing a play is mostly hard work. And in a professional production like *Really Rosie* that is what the actors are paid for—hard work. The usual work week for a play is eight hours a day, six days a week, plus the homework of learning lines and studying the play. Because of their ages and the fact that they would have to miss school during the weeks of rehearsal, the actors in *Really Rosie* worked six days a week, but rehearsals would begin for them at 10:00 A.M. and end at 4:00. A tutor would come in and help each of the cast keep up with schoolwork. When rehearsals ended and performances began, they would be back in school full time and performing at night.

In working on a play, memorizing the lines and learning the songs is the easy part. Almost anyone can do it. An actor's primary job in rehearsal is to create an interesting character and to bring to life the role he or she has been assigned to play.

In many productions, the cast will not sit down and read the play together again after the first reading. Most directors want to get the play on its feet as soon as possible, to get the actors moving on the stage or in the rehearsal hall. At this point the scenery, or background against which the play takes place, has not been put up yet. Instead, the stage manager marks off with tape a full-scale diagram on the stage floor so the director will not place the actors on any part of the stage that cannot be used once the scenery is in place. If the scenery includes furniture, some boxes or folding chairs might be used.

13

*Musical director Joel Silberman goes over a song
with actors Wade Raley (left) and Joey LaBenz.*

The movement of the actors on stage—where they sit, stand, lie down, and so forth—is called blocking and gives a play its shape. In blocking a play, the director breaks it down into a number of scenes and works on each one separately. A scene is worked on as long as it takes to bring it to life, and to achieve this the blocking may be changed every time the scene is rehearsed. The more difficult scenes will be worked on longer than the simpler ones, and the director will keep skipping around and building each scene separately and slowly.

Most directors will begin blocking a play as early in the rehearsal period as possible, but in a musical, songs and dances must be considered. Blocking of the musical portions must wait until the actors have learned their songs. So, in the beginning, the director will turn the cast over to the composer or musical director.

For *Really Rosie,* musical director Joel Silberman played the piano for the rehearsals, and during the first few days much of the time was spent with the cast grouped around the piano as Joel taught them their songs. Even so, Pat Birch began blocking the play on the morning of the second day.

When the director begins blocking, the stage manager is at the director's side at all times. As the director tells an actor on stage where to move, the stage manager makes a note of it in his or her script. The placement of every actor on the stage is written down so that if a scene has to be repeated there is no guessing where the actors should be. And, anytime the director changes the blocking, the old notes are erased and the new blocking is written in. By the time rehearsals end and the play opens, every page of the stage manager's script will be covered with notes.

After the play opens, the director will visit the play only once in a while, and it will become the stage manager's job to run the show on a day-to-day basis.

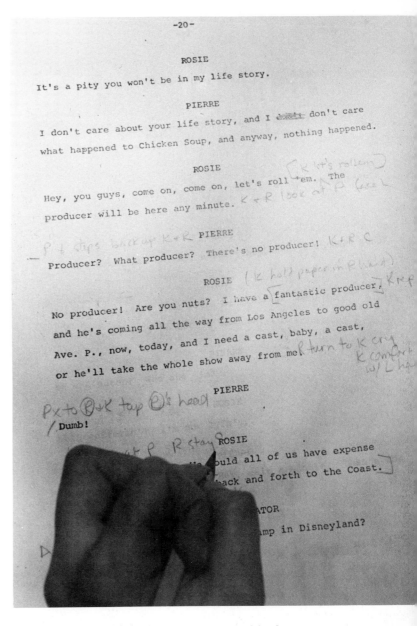

The stage manager writes down all the blocking, or movements of the actors on stage.

He or she will give instructions to the actors so that the director's staging will remain intact. And if, for any reason, an actor has to be replaced, the stage manager will be able to coach the new actor by referring to the notes in the script.

15

The first few weeks of rehearsal are mostly trial and error, with the actors and the director and, in a musical, the musical director and choreographer trying to find the best way to do a scene. It requires intense concentration and hard work. Scenes are repeated over and over as changes are made to perfect them.

April, Joey, Wade, and B. J. Barie follow Pat as she blocks in a scene.

Here is an example from *Really Rosie* of how director-choreographer Pat Birch, musical director Joel Silberman, and stage manager Janet Friedman worked with April Lerman in the musical number "The Awful Truth."

Joel sat at the piano, and Janet knelt with her script spread out on the stage, ready to help April if she forgot a line. Pat stood between the stage and the first row.

Joel began to play, and Pat let April dance by herself for a while as she watched. Then Pat got up on the stage and had April sit down. Pat began the song. "Close your eyes and visualize . . ." She hesitated. "LINE." Janet gave her the line. Pat talked her way through the song, with Janet feeding her the lines. Then Pat and April danced together, with Pat in front so that April could pick up her moves and copy them. April followed her perfectly. They backed up and did it again, Pat making changes as they danced. Joel played the piano hard, stressing the beat to help keep the dance in time. The dancers paused. Pat had April watch her again as she tried some new moves. Pat wanted to show a young girl's idea of a sexy dance, but she also had to limit the dance to things April could do. All the while, Janet was writing down the blocking as fast as her pencil would go.

Pat Birch teaches April a dance routine.

April got up and tried the dance, Joel following her closely. As they worked, Pat broke the dance into smaller and smaller pieces, to make the moves more specific, to make each moment clearer. They danced together again. The dance was built bit by bit. April stood and watched again. Pat was lying on her side with her left leg in the air, her foot pumping to the beat of Joel's piano. She broke off and went over to Joel. Pat stood by the piano, stomping her foot until she and Joel were in perfect time. Then she danced away from the piano as Joel watched her intently. Pat brought April back to the middle of the stage.

This is how April's song, "The Awful Truth," looked once the backdrop for the scene was in place.

They swayed together as Pat counted, "ONE, TWO, THREE, FOUR, FIVE, SIX, SEVEN, EIGHT, BA-BAA. ONE, TWO, THREE, FOUR, FIVE, SIX, SEVEN, EIGHT, BA-BAA." Over and over. April picked it up and danced by herself. The dance came alive. April was making it her own. Wrapped in an old blue bedspread, she did a sexy bump and grind and laughed at herself. The other three smiled. April continued the song. "I got the looks, I got the style. . ." Pat's voice was heard over hers, keeping the song and dance in time, "ONE, TWO, THREE, FOUR, ONE, TWO, THREE, FOUR," as April went on to finish the song.

Pat goes over motivation for a scene with Tisha Campbell and her brother, Jermaine.

After the first week of rehearsals, an actor usually knows all of his or her lines and songs and no longer has to carry a script on stage. It is then that the real work on the part can begin. Pat Birch and Tisha Campbell, who played Rosie, spent hours and hours just on Rosie's first speech in the play. Rosie is the main character. It is Rosie who helps the other kids on the street get through the long summer day. It is Rosie who must set the tone of the play. In her first speech and song, Rosie has to catch the audience's attention and get them interested—because if Rosie can't, the rest of the play will be in trouble.

23

Tisha and Pat go over a piece of stage business to make sure each movement seems spontaneous and unplanned.

Day after day, Tisha and Pat worked to find exactly the right way to begin. On some mornings Pat would have Tisha report for rehearsal an hour before the others and she and Joel Silberman would work with Tisha on her opening speech and song. They were still trying to improve the scene a few days before the play opened.

In rehearsals, saying the same lines over and over while working on a scene creates a difficult problem for an actor. Each time a scene is worked on, an actor must approach the words as if they had never been said before. He or she must listen to the other actors as if not knowing what they will say next. This is not easy, even for the best actors, but it is essential for the success of the play. Also, when an actor knows his or her part, the lines become so familiar to both the actor and the director that the lines are not really heard. During rehearsals Pat Birch kept reminding everyone in the cast that no matter how many times they said a line or how well they knew it, the audience would be hearing it for the first time. "And," she said, "if the audience doesn't hear it, you'll lose them."

B. J. Barie, who played Pierre, knew his lines well, but he was rushing them so much that no one could understand what he was saying. And, even though he brought great energy to the role, it was being wasted because he couldn't slow down. Pat had to get him to slow down and think of the meaning of each line before he said it.

With Janet referring to the script to make sure B.J. said his lines accurately, Pat stood in the middle of the theater with her back to him. She closed her eyes so that there would be no distractions. She called for B.J. to start. B.J. began his first line. Pat stopped him. "I didn't hear that. Again." B.J. began again. Pat stopped him again. "Do it again." Pat had him repeat his lines over and over. If he hesitated, Janet would call out the line. B.J. was getting angry with himself. But it worked. He was thinking about what he was saying and his lines were heard clearly.

B. J. Barie

*Maurice Sendak and Pat Birch discuss the script
and blocking with the cast.*

26

Pat works with the cast on staying in character during a song.

In blocking a play, the director does not spend an equal amount of time working on each scene and does not work in sequence. Because of this, it is difficult to know how well the scenes relate to one another. As soon as a large section of the play has been blocked in, the director will begin doing the scenes in order. This is called a run-through. A run-through might be a long section of the play, one act, or the entire play, depending upon how far rehearsals have progressed. After the first week or so, the rehearsal day is usually spent blocking new scenes, or reworking scenes that have already been blocked in, and then doing a run-through in the afternoon to review the work so far. This constant review is necessary to keep track of how the play is coming together.

Run-throughs are important because they give the director, the composer, and the playwright an opportunity to see if what was written comes alive on the stage. And when the scenes are strung together in a run-through, it is easier to see which ones work and which need more rehearsal time.

After a run-through, lines may be cut or new lines added, songs may be thrown out or rewritten, or new songs added. Almost any kind of change is possible. But a good director is cautious about making changes until it is absolutely necessary. Very often the key to making a scene work lies in the text of the play, so when things don't work, the director will go back, study the script, and try to find the answers in what the author has written.

27

As rehearsals progress, more and more props, or objects, appear on stage. Those used by the actors, such as a broom or dish towel, are the most important, so each one is assigned a place either on stage or backstage. It is part of the stage manager's job to make a list of all the props and to check that each is in its proper place before every rehearsal, run-through, or performance. During rehearsals it wastes time if a prop is misplaced when an actor needs it and during a performance it can be a disaster.

Stage manager Janet Friedman with one of the props used in the musical number "Pierre"

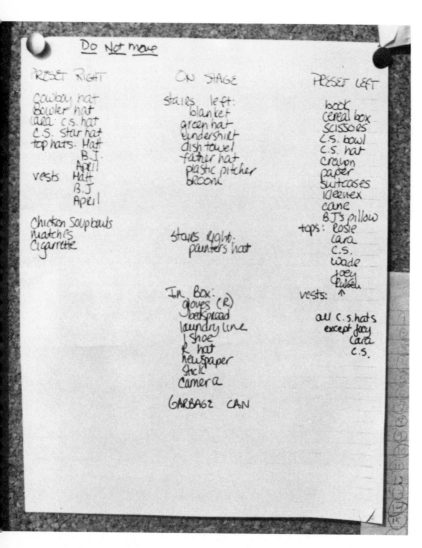

Before every performance the stage manager will go over the backstage checklist for costumes and props, to make sure everything is accounted for.

With the second week of rehearsals for *Really Rosie* coming to an end, there were already dozens of props to be accounted for. During a lunch break, stage manager Janet Friedman worked out the placement of all those needed so far. As the blocking of the play changed, so did the props. Some would disappear and others would be added.

The first two weeks of rehearsal are important to the director and cast because they are free of the technical problems that have to be dealt with when the lighting, scenery, and costumes are brought in. And as the time approaches to turn more attention to the technical side of the production, rehearsals become more intense. Concentration becomes all-important. Lack of attention to details, mistakes in blocking, or forgotten lines waste valuable time.

"Pierre" was one of the longest and most difficult of the musical numbers in *Really Rosie*. The blocking was very complicated. Added to this, there were quite a few props to be handled—a blanket; hats for Joey, Wade, and April; a cereal box; pitcher; garbage can, among others. In the scene, Tisha acts as storyteller as she sings the story of Pierre. The others act out the story and sing their parts. What made it so difficult was that the blocking had to match the action described in the lyrics. As the audience listened to Tisha, they would be watching the others. The timing had to be just right or the scene would not make sense.

"Pierre" was one of the most difficult numbers in the show.

Pat had planned the scene carefully, and she began working on it in small sections. Without putting music to the scene right away, she had the cast act out the story as Janet read the lyrics. But the long hours of rehearsal were beginning to tell. When Pat brought in the music, the scene would fall apart. Someone would forget an entrance, or the lyrics, or come in too early or too late. And although the cast was frustrated and tired, Pat had no choice but to keep them going until they got it right.

Toward the end of the second week, before they quit for the day, Pat sat the cast down for a talk. They had spent another morning working on "Pierre." They had just finished the afternoon run-through. It was no good and they knew it.

"Now, I'm very serious," Pat began. "What Sendak has written is terrific. What Carole King has written is terrific. And you were chosen because you have the talent and, I thought, the discipline to do something beautiful. A cast of kids doing a show, not just for kids, but for adults as well. There is no telling what we can do if we're good enough, and I will go to any cost to make it good." She paused. "So, whoever is not good enough in it, I will have to say good-bye to. I'm not saying this to threaten you. I'm simply telling you that's the way it is." She sent the cast home with instructions to rest and come in fresh the next day.

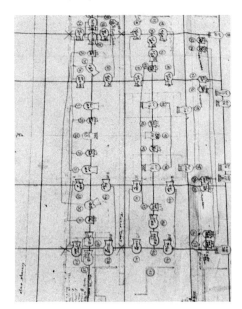

3

Lighting, Scenery, and Costumes

In a theater, the permanent lights that hang above the seats are called the house lights. Before the performance of a play, the house lights are slowly turned down and off and all the illumination for the play is created by the lighting designer.

Think of a room and what it looks like early in the morning, or in the afternoon, or late at night, or on a sunny day, or a dark, dreary one. A lighting designer can create all these effects in the theater by the way he or she uses lighting. But, what a lighting designer does depends on the play.

In *Really Rosie* most of the action takes place outside, on a city street in the middle of the summer. Lighting designer John Gleason had to give the street the look of daylight on a warm summer day. One scene in the play takes place in a dark cellar, when a sudden storm sends the kids there for shelter. With his lights Gleason created a flash of lightning and the cool gray light of the cellar. These and other effects were carefully planned, and the lighting to create them was included in Gleason's light plot weeks before rehearsals began.

A light plot is a diagram of how and where the lights are to be hung above the stage. After the lighting designer has read the play and discussed it with the director and the set designer, the light plot is drawn up and the lights are ordered from a company that rents out theatrical lighting supplies. The lights for *Really Rosie* were delivered to the Chelsea Theater during the second week of rehearsals. As Pat Birch and the actors were leaving the theater in the afternoon, the light crew began stacking the lights and cables on the stage and in the aisles of the theater. Head electrician Robin Cocking and her crew made trip after trip downstairs to the lobby to haul the one hundred lights and more than five thousand feet of cables up into the theater. Robin unfolded the light plot and spread it out on the stage to begin studying it.

The lighting equipment was delivered to the theater during the second week of rehearsals. The day it arrived, head electrician Robin Cocking (second from left) began to hang the lights.

Above the stage and the seats of the Chelsea Theater is a gridwork of pipes suspended about two feet from the ceiling. The lights were to be hung on these pipes. Before they began work, Robin instructed her crew that she wanted each length of cable labeled so that there would be no confusion. Then two tall extension ladders were brought on stage and the crew began stringing the cables. One end of each cable was tied to a pipe above the stage, and the cable was stretched along another pipe all the way back to the control booth at the rear of the theater. There the other end of the cable was connected to a control box. All the cables were strung this way and tied to the pipes in bundles.

Three members of the crew study the light plot. The colored gels that fit over each light are on the right.

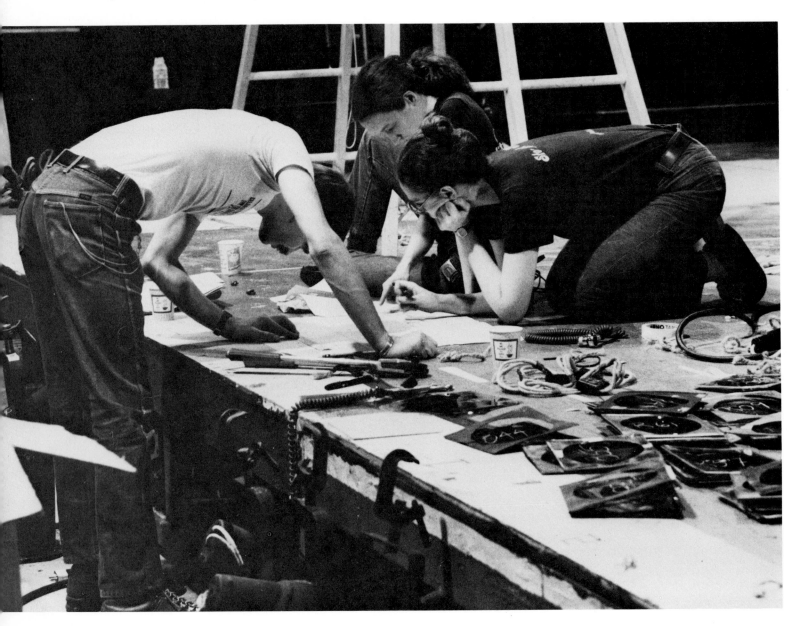

As each light was mounted above the stage and connected to a cable, a numbered gel was slipped in place. A gel is a small square of transparent colored plastic in a metal frame that fits over the front of a light to add color.

It took two nights to hang all the lights. The second night was a long one, but before Robin and her crew left the theater at 3:00 A.M., every light was in place and had been individually tested. There was still a lot of work to do before the lighting for the show was complete, but nothing more could be done until the scenery was in place.

On Sunday, September 21, John Gleason visited rehearsals for the first time to see how Pat Birch had blocked the play. As the afternoon run-through began, Gleason opened his script to follow the action of the play. He began making notes of where the actors sat or stood and especially where they were when they sang.

Just as the director would be able to focus the audience's attention by how and where she placed the actors on stage, Gleason would do it by his use of lighting. Together they would show the audience where to look. Say there are a dozen actors grouped together on stage and the stage is evenly lit. If one of the actors separates from the group our eyes will follow that actor. If the lighting changes so that the lone actor is in darkness and the group remains in the light, our eyes will shift back to the group. In a large theater and in a play with a large cast, focusing the audience's attention becomes more difficult.

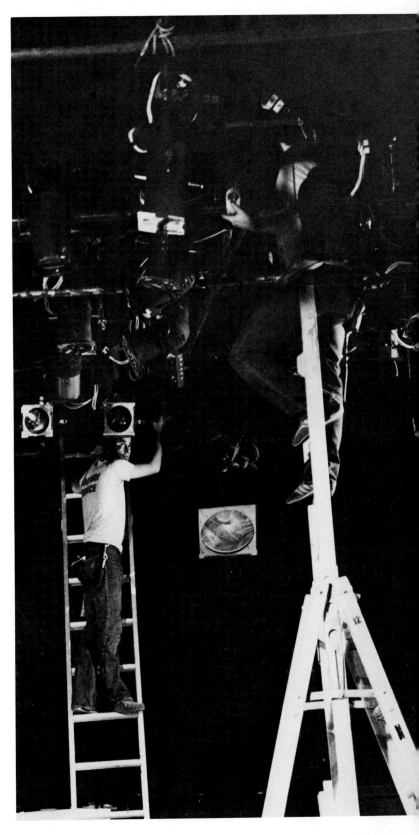

The lights are hung from a gridwork of pipes above the stage and seats.

The scenery of a play is the background against which the actors perform. It shows where the play takes place. It could be a room, or on board a ship or train, or, as in *Really Rosie,* a street. Scenery can be very realistic. A room can be built and furnished to look real enough to live in. At other times there may be real furniture, but the doors and windows might be painted on a canvas backdrop. And some plays will use no scenery at all.

The scenery for *Really Rosie* was designed by Maurice Sendak. Douglas Schmidt, set designer for dozens of Broadway plays, was hired to make Sendak's designs work in the space of the stage. He met with Sendak and Pat Birch weeks before rehearsals began. Then while Sendak did some preliminary designs, Doug Schmidt built a model of the inside of the Chelsea Theater to help Sendak see how his designs would look on stage.

Set supervisor Doug Schmidt and Pat Birch inspect the backdrops that have just arrived from Canada.

Pat Birch and Maurice Sendak

A series of backdrops, which hung like giant window shades, would be used to show where each scene takes place. Sendak did detailed paintings for these and delivered them to a scenery painting shop in Montreal, Canada. There the backdrops were painted on canvas, sixteen and a half feet high and from twenty-three to thirty-two feet wide.

Doug Schmidt also built a model of the set, and small copies of the four backdrops were fitted into it. The model was used by the director in planning the blocking. It was used by the carpenters and mechanics who would be building the set, and it gave the costume and lighting designers a feeling for what the set was going to look like.

He then drew up a series of blueprints, which are detailed drawings of each piece of scenery giving the dimensions for the set builder. The blueprints were sent to a shop that specializes in building scenery for plays, and just as rehearsals were getting under way, construction on the set for *Really Rosie* began.

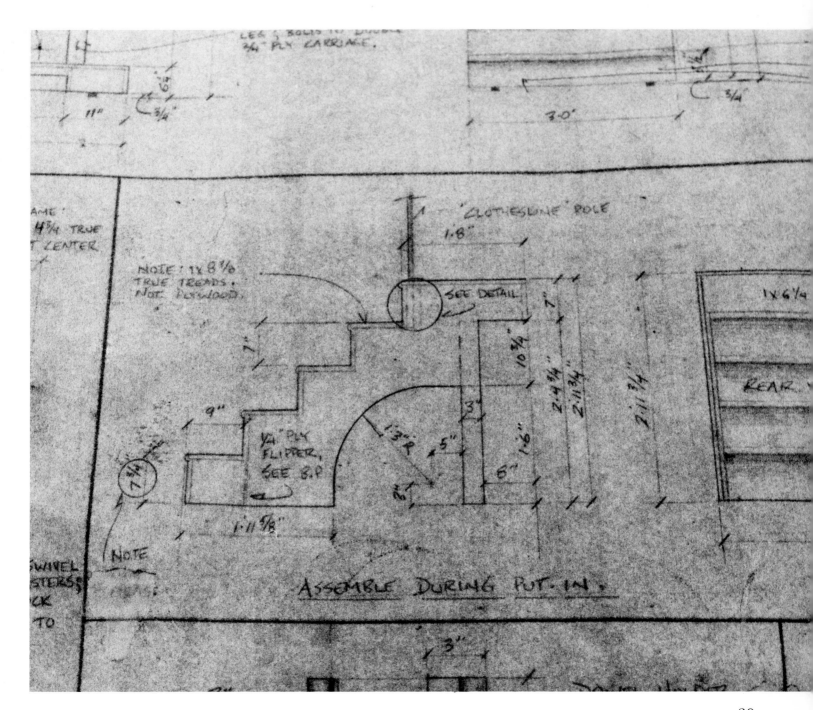

No matter how big a set is, it must be built in sections small enough to fit through the theater doors. As it is being built, the various sections are painted and assembled so it is certain they will fit together properly. If there is enough space, the entire set might be put together in the shop so the designer can see it and make any changes necessary. Then the set is dismantled and shipped to the theater. It is like building a house, taking it apart, and building it again in a new location. The set for *Really Rosie* was delivered to the theater on a Monday during the third week of rehearsals.

Construction on the set for Really Rosie *gets underway at a shop that specializes in building scenery for plays.*

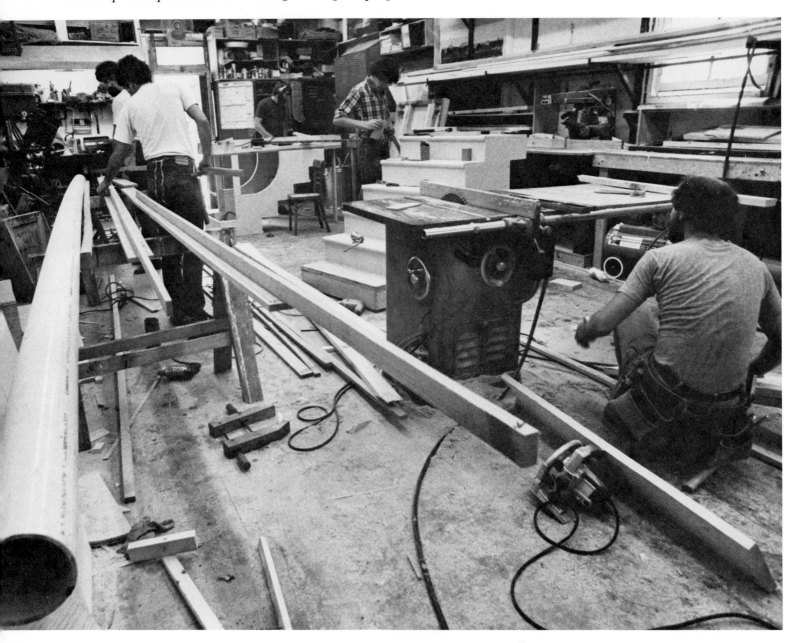

The set is loaded into the theater in sections small enough to fit through the theater doors.

New flooring is put down on the stage and painted a light gray. Later the lighting director found the floor reflected too much light, so it was painted dark blue.

The set is assembled on the stage of the Chelsea Theater.

On Tuesday the actors worked in a small rehearsal space downstairs while the set was being put together in the theater. The construction of the set was completed on Thursday afternoon, and the cast moved back upstairs. So far, they had to imagine the street where the play takes place.

Four days after the set was loaded into the theater, it was completely assembled. Tisha Campbell tries out her new "neighbornood."

Now it was in front of them—it would take time to get used to it. They hopped up on the stage and began trying it out.

The next seven days would be the most intense time in the rehearsal period. Before October 2, when the first paying audience would see the play, all the elements in the production would have to come together—actors, scenery, lighting, music, and costumes. Technical rehearsals would be held to see how the actors and the set worked together. The cast would run through the play without really acting. They would move through all the blocking they had learned, but they would be told to forget about their characters temporarily. It would be a time for the playwright, director, and the designers to see if their plans were working and to make any changes that would help the play.

Now that the set is in place, a technical rehearsal will be held to focus the lights.

When the actors left the theater Thursday afternoon, Gleason walked onto the stage to begin focusing the lights. One of the light crew mounted a tall ladder and waited for instructions from Gleason before adjusting the lights. After consulting his light plot, Gleason called for each one by number. The light was turned on and carefully directed to the exact spot Gleason wanted. The beam of light could be made to take the shape of a circle, square, triangle, or rectangle. To light up one of the windows on the set, Gleason had the technician adjust the shutters in the light to fit the shape of the window exactly. The brightness, or dimmer level, of each light would be adjusted the next day.

Lighting director John Gleason points to part of the scenery. He wants the technician adjusting the lights to avoid letting the light spill off it.

Gleason directs the lighting with his fingers.

Gleason stands on the spot the light should be aimed at.
When the beam hits him directly in the eyes, it will be
right where he wants it.

On Friday John Gleason, Pat Birch, and Doug Schmidt sat together during the run-through. It was stop and go all day as Gleason set the light levels. Each time he made an adjustment, the actors had to stand still on the stage. It was as if they were posing for a long series of pictures.

Each signal for a change in lighting during a play is called a light cue. The lighting designer makes a note of all the light cues in the play and gives them to the stage manager and the electrician who controls the lights in the control booth. The stage manager then marks down in his or her script when each light cue takes place, and the electrician makes a chart, listing the light cues and dimmer levels in order.

During a performance the lighting is constantly changing, although most of the time the changes are hardly noticeable because they are done so slowly. The stage manager calls out each light cue to the electrician as it comes up in the script, and the electrician changes the lighting. However, until the play opens, the light cues, like everything else, are subject to change.

In the control booth at the back of the theater, electrician David Crist watches the stage as he changes the lighting.

Maurice Sendak designed the costumes for Really Rosie.

One morning during the first week of rehearsals Pat Birch sat down with Wade Raley to discuss Johnny, the character he was playing.

"Wade, what is Johnny like?"

Wade tilted his head to the side and said, "He's a snobby and scientific kid."

"What does he look like?" asked Pat.

"He might wear glasses."

"Do you want to wear glasses?"

"No," said Wade.

But he had said the right thing. In Sendak's sketches Johnny does wear glasses. Pat sent Janet backstage to find a pair for Wade.

After studying the play and consulting with the director and playwright, the costume designer will make sketches for the costumes, taking the scenery into consideration, so that the actors will not blend in with the set. He or she must also make sure the costumes in some way reflect the characters the actors are playing. For *Really Rosie,* Sendak supplied sketches of the costumes based on the characters in his books. Carrie Robbins, a well-known costume designer, had the job of creating or buying clothes that would match the clothes worn by Sendak's characters.

Except for Tisha's, almost all of the costumes for *Really Rosie* were bought. Carrie Robbins's assistant, Ticia Blackburn, attended the first day of rehearsal and took measurements of everyone in the cast. Then she began shopping.

All during the first three weeks Ticia came into rehearsals and, during a break, had the kids try on the sneakers, shirts, and jeans she had bought. She and Carrie were trying to be as faithful to Sendak's drawings as they possibly could. As Carrie put it, "We have an obligation to the man."

It took a lot of shopping to find the right clothes. They were then altered and washed over and over so they wouldn't look new, dyed a different color if necessary, or painted to look worn.

The vests used in the play had to be "built." In the language of the theater, costumes are built, not made.

At the costumer's, Tisha Campbell stretches in her new jeans. They had to be cut off above the knees so she could move more freely.

*Tisha tries on her veil
while the legs of her
jeans are cut off.*

53

In the play, Rosie is the leader of her small circle of friends. She is imaginative and leads a crowded fantasy life, with dreams of Hollywood movies. In her bright red dress, long gloves, and big hat with feathers she is a star, and Sendak's sketches reflected this. But there were some differences between the sketches and the finished costume.

Because Tisha was so active on stage, the brim of her hat had to be pinned back.

Sendak's sketch of Rosie's costume made sense as a drawing, but Carrie had to make some adjustments for it to work on stage. The sketch showed the dress touching the floor and dragging behind Rosie, with long feathers flowing out of her floppy hat. But Tisha, who had to run, jump, and dance in her costume, could not wear a dress that long, and when she threw her arms up she knocked her hat off the first time she wore it. In the final version of the costume the feathers remained but they were looped around and tied to the hat and the dress was pinned so it was off the floor.

At the costumer's Tisha met with Carrie and her assistant for the final fitting of her dress. The dress looked too big, but in reality it fit Tisha perfectly. Fake tucks had been made in the red satin and large safety pins were pushed through the material to make it look like they were holding the dress off the ground. Carrie had Tisha kick her legs and dance. Her legs moved freely.

When selecting the material for a costume, Carrie often consults with the lighting designer to see what color gels are to be used during the play. She then covers two floodlights at the costumer's with the same color gels so she can see what the costume will look like on stage. Even with all the planning, changes might still have to be made when the director sees the costume on stage, under the lights, and in front of the scenery during the dress rehearsal.

Costume supervisor Carrie Robbins explains where she wants Tisha's red dress pinned.

CHAPTER

4

The Music

The entire cast of *Really Rosie* was made up of very young actors, most of whom could not read music. They had to learn the songs by ear. To speed up the process, musical director Joel Silberman used the following technique during the first week of rehearsals to help Wade Raley learn his long solo in "One Was Johnny."

Joel sang while Wade listened and followed the lyrics in his script. Then Wade sang with Joel guiding him through the song. Next, Joel sang a short section and Wade repeated it. They went through the entire song this way. Then Joel made a tape of Wade singing so Wade could take it home and study it.

A few days later, when Wade was sure of the lyrics, another tape was made. This time Wade and Joel sang together. The purpose of the new tape was to help Wade hit the proper notes. This method was used only for the solos. When the entire cast sang, Joel had to teach them their parts during rehearsal, which meant a lot of time at the piano.

Wade Raley listens for mistakes as the tape recorder
plays back his recording of "One Was Johnny."

*Joel Silberman works with the cast on a song. Unless all
the voices are heard, the harmony will be destroyed.*

Joel teaches the cast some breathing exercises. The strain
of rehearsals was beginning to show in their singing.

The score for the musical number "Chicken Soup with Rice"

The music for the play was written for the piano. Music for the other instruments had to be written also, but most composers do not have the necessary skills for this, so the task of expanding the score is usually assigned to a musical arranger.

For *Really Rosie,* Joel Silberman did the arrangements. After teaching the cast the songs, he was ready to begin working on the arrangements, but first he had to see how Pat Birch was going to stage each musical number. While Pat Birch was staging the songs, Joel began making notes in his score to indicate how and where he wanted the other instruments to play. If the song was a

60

Meredith Marcellus copies the parts for the different instruments while Joel works on the arrangements.

solo, the band had to play softly enough so the singer could be heard. But if it was sung by a chorus, the whole band could be used and the sound could be much fuller. Because Joel could not work on the arrangements until the songs were staged, when he did start he had to work furiously to get them finished on time.

When all the parts for all the instruments were written, they were turned over to a copyist. The copyist would copy the music for each instrument by hand on separate musical sheets so that every musician would have a score.

Really Rosie *used a small backstage band.*

Joel and Meredith rush to finish their work on the arrangements in time for the band's first rehearsal with the actors.

Really Rosie used a small backstage band of five musicians, including Joel, who conducted from the piano. The five musicians played a total of nine instruments. Even for this small group, the job done by Joel's assistant, Alex Rybeck, and copyist Meredith Marcellus, was a huge one. There were eleven musical numbers for the nine instruments, which meant that ninety-nine different parts had to be copied.

Using the songs in the show, Joel also had to compose an overture, which is the music played just before the curtain rises and the show begins. The overture is meant to reflect the spirit of the play and put the audience in the right mood. Joel worked hard to create an exciting one, and just after he finished writing it, he described it to Alex one day during a lunch break.

Alex was looking at the music over Joel's shoulder as Joel began to play. Over the sound of the piano Joel called out where he wanted the other instruments to play. "It's piccolo to there . . . saxophone to here . . . saxophone through there . . . piano . . . and I want to come in with the clarinet here." Joel pointed to the score. "Yah, bah, da, bah . . . guitar . . . di, dadi, da . . . sax and piano . . . this will be just rhythm section to give him [the sax player] time to pick up the flute." Alex began to whistle the flute part. Joel was happy with what he had written. The overture came to an end. "All right," said Joel. Alex applauded.

In addition to songs and dance music and the overture, most musicals, like movies, have music to underscore, or emphasize, the mood of certain scenes.

In one scene in *Really Rosie* the children run off and leave Rosie. Kathy is the last to leave and she feels bad because she is leaving her best friend alone As the actors played the scene and said good-bye, Joel used the music from one of Kathy's songs to underscore the action, which added greatly to the feeling of the scene.

In one scene, Kathy, played by April Lerman, had to say good-bye to her friend Rosie. When Joel underscored the action with music the scene became very touching.

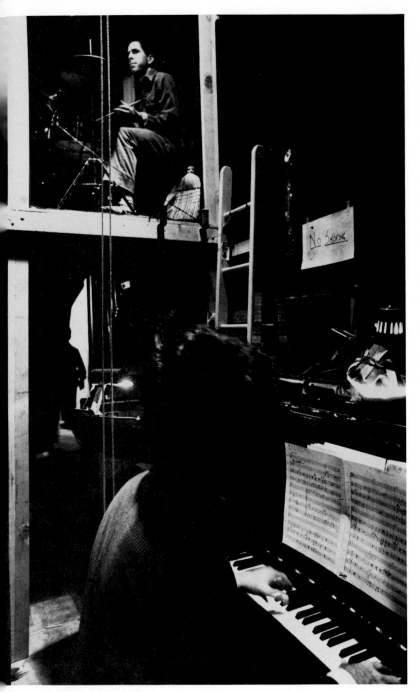

One of the major problems faced in the production of any musical is getting the proper balance between the singers and the orchestra. On Sunday, September 28, two nights after Joel had begun rehearsing the band, a problem surfaced that took almost two weeks to clear up. Some of the songs were completely drowned out and the singers could not be heard.

Most productions in large theaters use microphones to amplify the singers' voices, which allows the orchestra to play the way it must to make the music sound right. But this means hiring a sound expert to balance the sound electronically.

Microphones and amplifiers were not brought in for *Really Rosie*. Instead, Joel experimented by substituting different instruments and by altering his arrangements, which, of course, meant more work for the copyist. The balance was found, but that Sunday night during the run-through the solution seemed far away.

Joel makes changes in the arrangements.

Joel and Pat discuss the musical arrangements backstage.

Monday, September 29, was dress rehearsal. For the first time, three days before an audience would see the show, the actors were in their costumes, on stage, in front of the scenery, and under the lights. Right away, it was decided that the green of Joey's costume was too bright. It would have to be dyed again. B.J.'s costume looked too clean. Ticia Blackburn took them away to be worked on some more.

The next few days would be used to tighten up the show and clean up technical problems before the previews began.

When B.J. wore his T-shirt for the first time it looked too clean.

A few days later it looked more in character.

B.J. tries on his vest for the dress rehearsal.

In his Alligator hat and green overalls, Joey waits on stage to be inspected.

Curtain calls have to be rehearsed. These versions never worked well and were dropped.

Pat leads the cast in a rehearsal of the curtain call that was used.

CHAPTER

5

Previews

There is a tradition on Broadway of rehearsing a play in New York, taking it out of town for a tryout, working out any problems, and then returning to New York for opening night. But moving a show costs a lot of money. And although it is still done with some shows, especially when a star is involved, many plays have their tryouts in New York. The producers call them previews.

Previews are performances that are used to test a play in front of a paying audience. They tell if the play works as planned, what changes would make it better, and, more important, whether the audience likes it or not. The ability to see what works in a play and to fix what doesn't is the mark of a good director. However, after weeks of rehearsals and having scenes and musical numbers repeated over and over, it is hard to see things with a fresh eye. The audience can point the way.

Right before curtain time, Pat talks quietly with Jermaine and Wade.

Pat and Tisha work on the opening speech in the play while stagehands prepare for the evening performance.

During previews, songs may be taken out of the show or new songs added. Dialogue may be cut or rewritten, whole scenes removed or rearranged. New scenery may have to be built, dances added, reworked, or thrown out. Costumes may be redesigned, and, of course, all these things may affect the lighting and the musical arrangements. When things look really bad, the director may be replaced. And if the producers decide the show isn't worth saving, they will close it before it opens.

This didn't happen with *Really Rosie*, but there were changes. The first preview was on the night of October 2. Almost every day after that, rehearsals were held before each performance to correct what went wrong the night before. This didn't end until opening night. What follows are some of the changes that took place.

72

Friday, October 3—Pat Birch reblocked the opening scene. This meant new light cues. John Gleason passed them on to the stage manager.

Saturday, October 4—The musical director, Joel Silberman, replaced the electric guitar in the band with an acoustic guitar. He replaced the tenor saxophone with a soprano one. New music had to be copied while Joel completed the new arrangements.

Sunday, October 5—Sendak sent in some new lines. Pat gave the cast new blocking. A drummer was hired for the band. He watched the performance and took notes.

Monday, October 6—A day off for the actors. A work crew came in. There was so little room backstage for the band that a platform had to be built for the drummer.

Tuesday, October 7—New lines were added, others cut. Pat gave the cast new blocking for the added lines. Jermaine was given a new costume. The drummer joined the band.

Wednesday, October 8—Sendak cut some more lines.

Thursday, October 9—A day off.

Friday, October 10—Joel held an extra band rehearsal. Emergency repairs had to be made on the set.

After a preview performance, the producers, director, and the costume, lighting, and scenery people discuss the work that has to be done before opening night.

Five minutes before every preview performance, Pat gathered the cast backstage for a pep talk.

Saturday, October 11—A day of crisis. Tisha and Jermaine were stuck in traffic on their way in from New Jersey. Even so, the rest of the cast took their places in the front row of the theater so Pat could go over her list of missed cues and lines not heard. The list went on and on. The cast was startled by its length. Pat held up the script. "Look for yourself," she said. After they were through, Pat had the kids hop up on stage to work on the "Chicken Soup with Rice" number. Tisha and Jermaine were still out on Route 4.

After lunch Janet Friedman called up to the electrician in the control booth. "David, let's do a fast light check." With her script in hand, Janet moved around the stage stepping in and out of the beams of light as David Crist changed the dimmer levels. The cast joined Joel at the piano for a voice warm-up.

Janet checked her watch. Without Tisha and Jermaine, the show would have to be canceled, but until that decision was made, everything had to be ready to go. At one-thirty Janet announced there was half an hour left before curtain time. The actors broke away from the piano and headed for the dressing rooms. The opening of the theater was held up. There was no point in seating the audience if the show had to be canceled. Fifteen minutes before curtain time, Tisha and Jermaine roared into the theater and dashed for their costumes. The theater was opened and the customers spilled in.

The matinee performance was down. The energy was down. It was a bad show. After getting out of their costumes, the cast drifted into the theater and lined up in the front row. Pat sat on the stage and looked up and down the row. "Kids, I find myself pointing out the same mistakes." She paused. "What can I do? What would you do?"

Silence.

"You're not thinking." Pat stood up. "I've done everything I could. It's in your hands now."

There wasn't a sound. Janet broke the silence. "Be back here at six-thirty."

Then Pat said, "Kids, tonight, let's do it for Maurice. He's written a wonderful play."

At some point in the rehearsal period, during a run-through or later during the previews, it suddenly happens. The actors take over the play. They take the play out of the hands of the playwright and the composer, the designers, and the director who has guided them, and make it theirs. This has to happen if a show is to be successful. The performers on stage are the ones the audience sees. The words they speak and the songs they sing must sound like their words, their songs, not something they were taught. The action on stage has to seem like it is happening for the first time. And, in a good production of a good play, it always does.

It happened in *Really Rosie* during the second week of previews. When Pat Birch gathered the cast in the front row after the performance on October 12, she said, "It was a good show. I have a few notes, but I'll give them tomorrow." She looked up and down the line and added, "The show is yours."

Monday, October 13—Pat had the cast do a double time run-through. The play went like a speeded-up movie. She was trying to keep things fresh and help the cast stay loose now that they were performing the play so well.

CHAPTER

6

Opening Night

October 14, 7:00 P.M.—Steve Boyle, one of the backstage crew, was sweeping up some sawdust from the latest repair work on the set. Gayle Palmieri, the wardrobe mistress, hurried across the stage and headed for the dressing rooms with costumes she had just picked up from the cleaners. Steve finished sweeping and put the broom away as stage manager Janet Friedman walked on stage. She glanced at her watch and then pointed out a light overhead to electrician David Crist, who was dragging a long extension ladder on stage. David climbed the ladder to replace a torn gel.

Assistant stage managers Bibi Humes and Alison Price were placing the props under the steps on stage—hats, a small pitcher, and a dish towel. Alison draped a blanket and Rosie's boa over the small clothesline and plopped Rosie's hat on one of the poles. They moved behind the scenery and checked the prop table backstage. Gayle Palmieri came back upstairs, her arms loaded with satin top hats and spangled vests for the finale. Because of the quick costume changes during the finale, these hung on the back of the scenery, just off the stage.

David Crist put the ladder away and returned to the control booth where he would be operating the lights. Janet Friedman picked up her script and called up to him. "David, let's do a light check." David waved to her and she began calling out the numbers. They went through all the lights in the show one by one, to be sure they were working and focused where they should be.

Musical director Joel Silberman had the band in early for a few last-minute changes. Small snatches of music rang out in the empty theater as a background for Janet's light show. When she reached the last light change, Janet called out, "Check. Thank you, David. You can go to preset." Janet moved off the stage and picked up the

The opening night audience

backstage microphone clipped to the wall. It was 7:30 P.M. "Half hour. Half hour. Kids, please sign in and go to your dressing rooms." She put the mike down and headed backstage.

Janet entered the girls' dressing room. The place was electric. Small, opening night gifts were lined up in front of the mirrors. Opening night party clothes were hanging neatly on a rack. Gayle Palmieri was trying valiantly to work on April's hair as she moved around excitedly. Tisha, already in costume, knelt on her chair waiting for Gayle to do her hair. Understudy Lara Berk sat in her chair, beaming at herself in the mirror. Janet interrupted them. "Girls, give me your attention. I have just a few small notes."

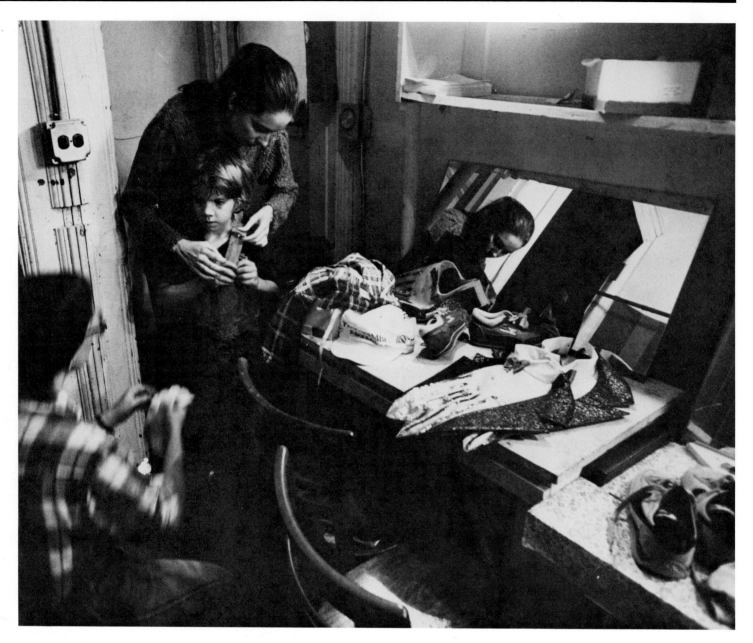

Ticia Blackburn helps Joey into his costume.

If the girls' dressing room was electric, the boys' was bedlam. Wade sat on the floor pulling on his socks. Joey was half-dressed, sitting on his dressing table. B.J., in bare feet, couldn't find his shoes. All three were yelling at each other. Ruben sat quietly amazed. Assistant stage manager Bibi Humes entered to speed up the dressing. "We don't want no girls in here," Joey yelled. Janet entered and gave her notes over the noise.

Janet returned to the stage. She looked at her watch and called out into the theater to the house manager. "Okay, you can open the house." Customers trickled in as Janet went to the backstage mike. "Fifteen minutes, please. Fifteen minutes." Joel and the band continued to rehearse as Janet made a final backstage inspection to be sure all the props were in their proper places.

Gayle was now in the boys' dressing room checking the costumes. Everyone was ready. The boys heard Janet's voice over the loudspeaker. "Five minutes, please. Five minutes." They tumbled out of the room to join the girls and their director. They joined hands and Pat Birch gave them some words of encouragement and a gentle warning. "Remember, if you make a mistake, don't worry about it. Once it's done, go on. You can't fix it. So don't try. Just go on." The kids nodded. "Now go out there and knock their blocks off."

Janet interrupted them. "Places. Let's go, kids. Places." The actors moved out to take their positions on either side of the stage. Pat hurried to her seat in the audience. The band was warming up. The muffled sound of chatter from the packed house came through the roll of the drums and the picking of the base guitar. Janet hurried to the control booth to join David. Assistant stage manager Alison Price put on her headset and waited for Janet's voice from the booth. Janet and David put on their headsets. Then, in the reassuring voice all good professional stage managers use, Janet said, "Let me know when you're ready." After a few moments, Alison answered that all was ready backstage, and Janet made her announcement.

In the lighting control booth, David Crist waits for a cue from the stage manager before the play begins.

"Ladies and gentlemen, boys and girls, welcome to *Really Rosie*. We'd like to remind you that the taking of pictures and the use of recording devices is strictly prohibited. Thank you." Janet called to David. "House to half." She flipped a switch to cue the band. A red light flashed in front of Joel. As the house lights dimmed, Joel raised his hands above his head and counted, "ONE, TWO, THREE, FOUR," and he gave the downbeat. The band swung into the overture.

Backstage in the semidarkness, Gayle knelt in front of Joey and adjusted one of the straps on his overalls. Joey moaned. "I didn't say good luck to one person." Tisha sat quietly on stage and listened to the overture. Gayle finished with the strap and Joey put on his Alligator hat and stood in the wings. As the end of the overture approached, Tisha got into position and straightened her dress. Janet flicked on the signal light for the curtain. With their eyes glued to the backstage light, stagehands Steve Boyle and Henry Sutro reached up and grabbed the curtain rope. Janet called to David. "Standby for cue two." David's fingers rested on the dimmer switches. Tisha stood poised. Bob Weiner began the drum roll that ended the overture. Janet flipped off the curtain light. "Cue two . . . go." Steve and Henry hauled up the curtain as David pushed the dimmer switches forward. A golden light bathed Tisha as she stepped forward to greet it. The light spilled into the wings and caught Lara's dimpled face locked in a delighted grin. Tisha stood downcenter, spread her arms and began to sing, "I'm really Rosie. . . ."

And she really was.

Backstage, Henry Sutro and Steve Boyle get ready to raise the curtain.

CHAPTER
7
Who's Who Behind the Scenes

arranger—writes the parts for the different instruments in the orchestra, based on the composer's work.

casting agent—finds actors suitable for the roles in the play and sends them to the auditions.

choreographer—creates the dances in the play and teaches them to the cast.

composer—writes the music for the play, usually for the piano.

copyist—copies by hand enough sets of music for all the instruments once it is written by the arranger.

costume designer—plans the clothing each actor will wear on stage.

costumer—makes or "builds" the costumes that are not bought.

director—oversees the entire production; mainly responsible for rehearsing the actors.

electrician—"hangs" or puts up the lights and focuses them for the lighting designer.

house manager—supervises the ushers and box office and sees that the theater is ready for each performance.

lighting designer—creates a plan for the lighting in the play.

lyricist—writes the words to the songs.

musical director—teaches the songs to the cast and conducts the orchestra during performances; may also write the musical arrangements.

playwright—the author of the play.

press agent—publicizes the play by getting news about it in print and on the radio and TV.

producer—raises the money for the play and hires the people necessary to produce it.

production electrician—supervises the hanging of the lights above the stage; during performances makes lighting changes from the control booth.

production supervisor—helps the producer and director coordinate the creative and technical aspects of the production.

scenery painter—paints the backdrops, usually based on art provided by the set designer.

set builder—constructs the scenery and installs it in the theater.

set designer—plans the scenery for the play.

stagehand—a backstage crew member responsible for making scenery changes; may also raise and lower the curtain.

stage manager—assists the director during rehearsals and runs the show after opening night.

understudy—an actor hired to substitute for another as necessary.

wardrobe person—takes care of the costumes and assists the actors in the dressing rooms before performances.

The Author

Bill Powers brings to *Behind the Scenes of a Broadway Musical* his own background in the theater and his work as a professional photographer and writer. He founded and directed the Second Story Players, an Off-Off-Broadway theater group that won the coveted Obie Award in 1967. Mr. Powers's photographs have appeared in many books and national magazines. He photographed *The Aran Islands* by Dennis Smith and has written two novels for young people. Born in Brooklyn, Bill Powers now lives in Manhattan with his wife, actress Patricia Powers.